Folk Song Primer

A Very Easy Book of Folk Songs
For Piano or Electronic Keyboard
By Wesley Schaum

T0078688

Foreword

This book is designed to make familiar folk songs as easy as possible. A student with just six to eight weeks study will be able to start enjoying this album.

The pieces are arranged in five-finger position with melody divided between the hands. A minimum of finger numbers is used. Large, widely spaced notes help make music reading easier. Rests have been purposely omitted so the student can focus on the notes.

Duet accompaniments offer many possibilities for recitals and Sunday school participation. The duets help provide rhythmic training and ensemble experience especially valuable to beginners. The person playing the accompaniment is free to add pedal according to his/her own taste.

The duets are recommended for use at home as well as at the lesson. However, the student should work alone at first until the notes and rhythm of the solo part are secure.

Index

EXCLUSIVELY DISTRIBUTED BY

HAL•LEONARD®
CORPORATION

7777 W. BLUEMOUND RD. P.O. BOX 13819 MILWAUKEE, WI 53213

© Copyright 1976 by Schaum Publications, Inc., Mequon, Wisconsin • International Copyright Secured • All Rights Reserved • Printed in U.S.A.
ISBN-13: 978-1-936098-84-2

Eency Weency Spider

American Folk Song

Vivace

mf Een - cy ween - cy spi - der went up the wa - ter spout.*

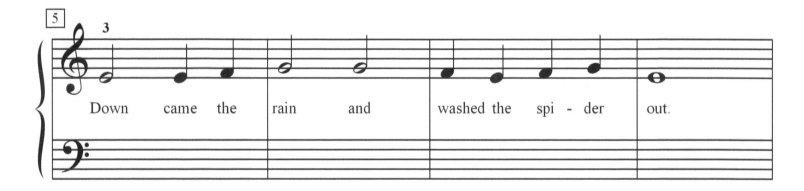

Down came the rain and washed the spi - der out.

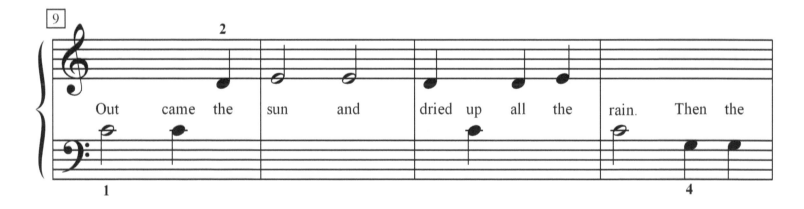

Out came the sun and dried up all the rain. Then the

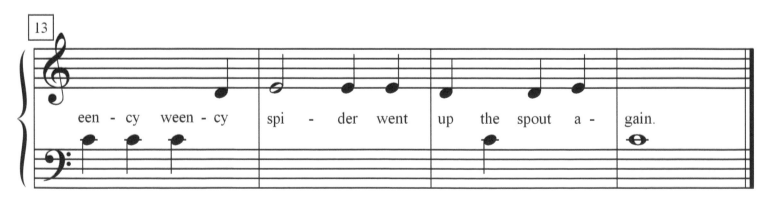

een - cy ween - cy spi - der went up the spout a - gain.

* A *water spout* is a drain pipe for rain water from a roof.

Duet Accompaniment (Stem up = R.H. Stem down = L.H.)

mf

Down in the Valley

Espressivo

American Folk Song

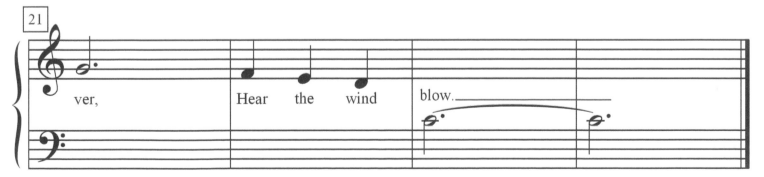

Duet Accompaniment

* Measure numbers in a square are for the first time through. Numbers in a circle are for the second time through.

Bear Went Over the Mountain

Allegro

Traditional

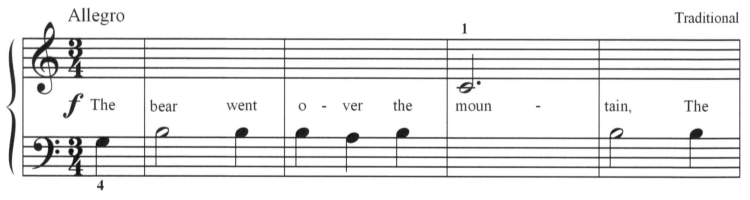

The bear went o - ver the moun - tain, The

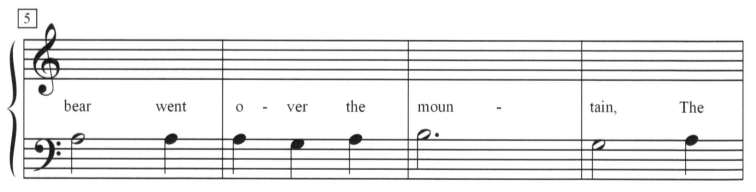

bear went o - ver the moun - tain, The

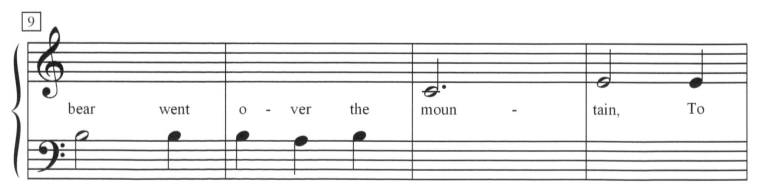

bear went o - ver the moun - tain, To

Duet Accompaniment

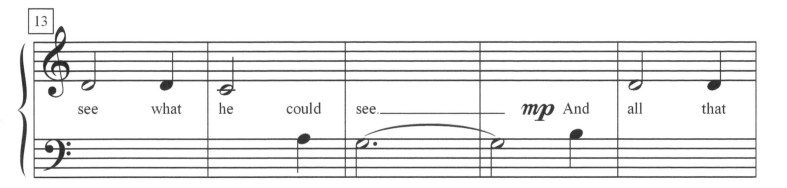

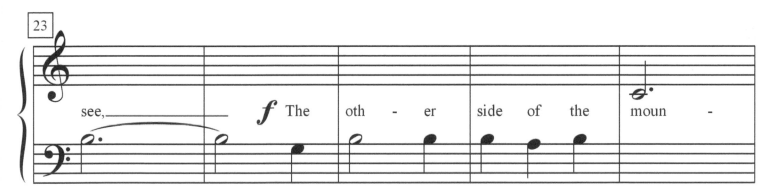

Duet Accompaniment (continued)

Shortnin' Bread

American Folk Song

Cockles and Mussels

Moderato

Old Irish Song

In Dub - lin's* fair cit - y where girls are so pret - ty, 'Twas

there I first met with sweet Mol - ly Ma - lone. She

drove a wheel - bar - row through streets wide and nar - row, Sing - ing

"Cock - les* and mus - sels, a - live, a - live oh!"

* *Dublin* is the capital and largest city in Ireland. *Cockles* and *mussels* are shellfish like clams and oysters.

Duet Accompaniment

Lil' Liza Jane

Animato

American Folk Song

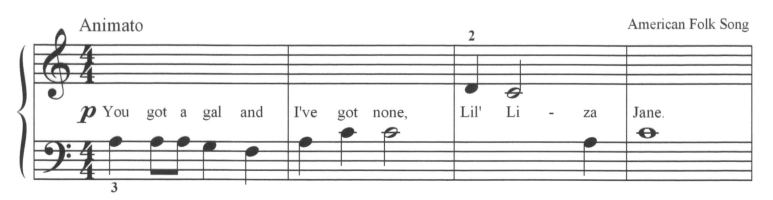

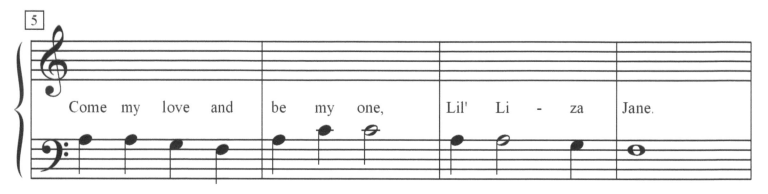

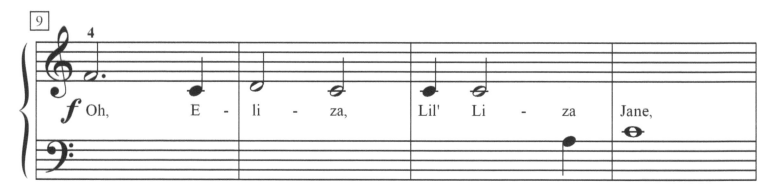

Duet Accompaniment

O Where Has My Little Dog Gone?

Giocoso

German Folk Song

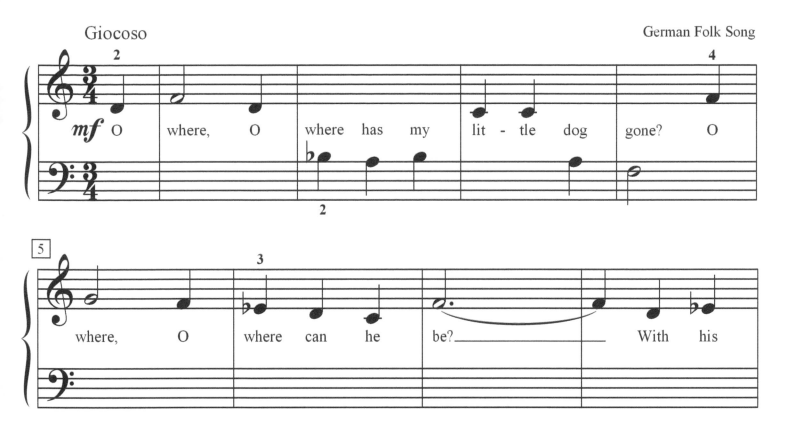

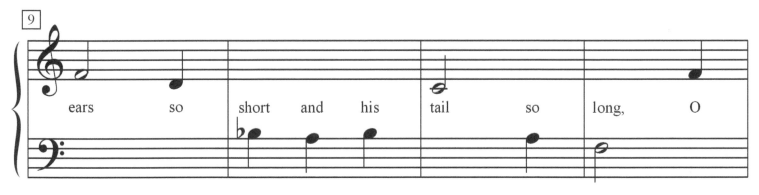

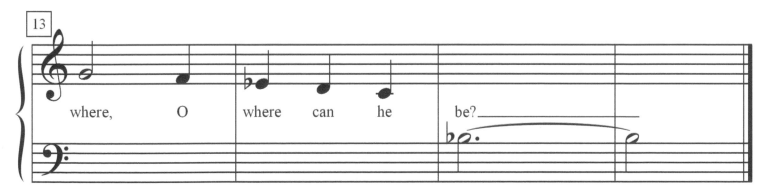

Duet Accompaniment

Sweet Betsy from Pike

American Folk Song

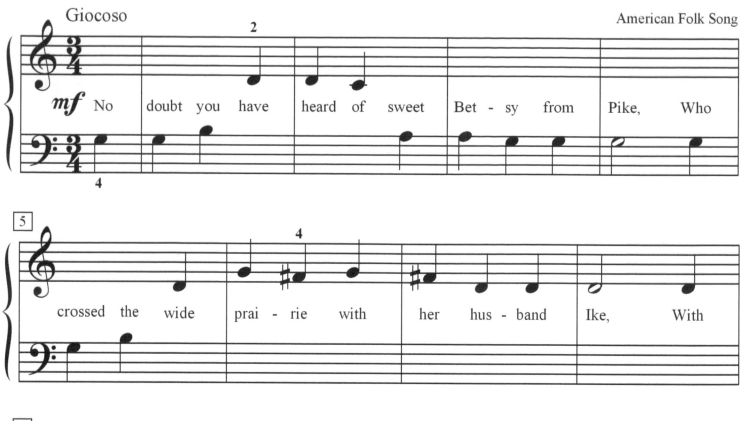

Giocoso

mf No doubt you have heard of sweet Bet - sy from Pike, Who

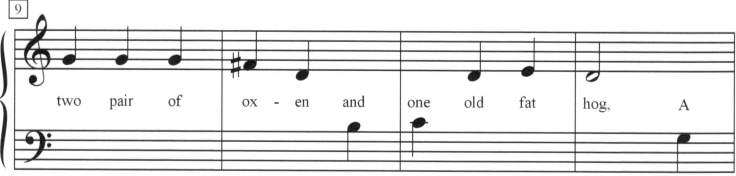

crossed the wide prai - rie with her hus - band Ike, With

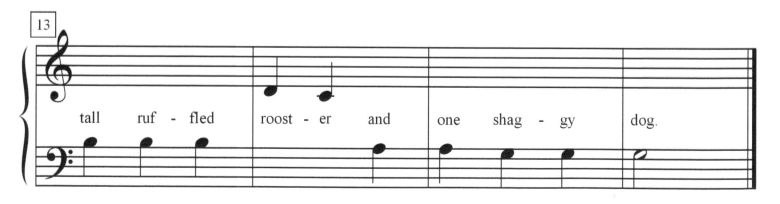

two pair of ox - en and one old fat hog, A

tall ruf - fled roost - er and one shag - gy dog.

Duet Accompaniment

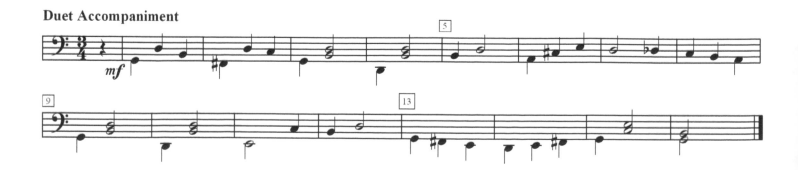

Skip to My Lou

Vivace

American Folk Song

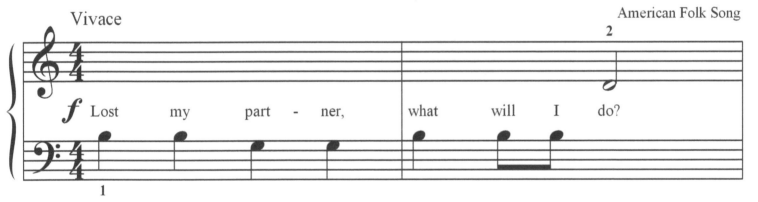

Lost my part - ner, what will I do?

Lost my part - ner, what will I do? I'll find an - oth - er

bet - ter than you, Skip to my Lou, my dar - lin'.

* *Lou* means "sweetheart" or "lover."

Duet Accompaniment

12

Shoo Fly

Allegro

Frank Campbell

Shoo fly, don't both - er me! Shoo fly, don't both - er me!

Shoo fly, don't both - er me! I be - long to Com-pa-ny G!*

Gol - ly, wow, I feel, I feel like a morn - ing star.*

Gol - ly, wow, I feel, I feel like a morn - ing star.

* This song originated during the American Civil War. *Company G* was a unit of the army.
The *morning star,* a symbol of brightness and happiness, appears in the early morning sky.

Duet Accompaniment

Little David Play on Your Harp

Con anima

Spiritual

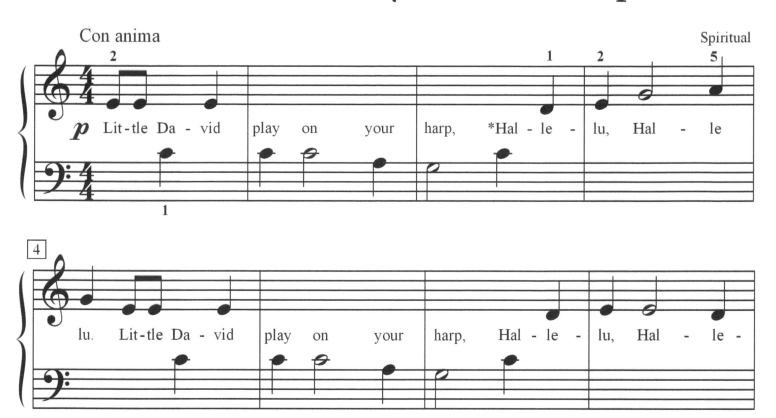

Lit-tle Da - vid play on your harp, *Hal - le - lu, Hal - le

lu. Lit-tle Da - vid play on your harp, Hal - le - lu, Hal - le -

lu. Lit-tle Da - vid play on your harp, Hal - le - lu, Hal - le -

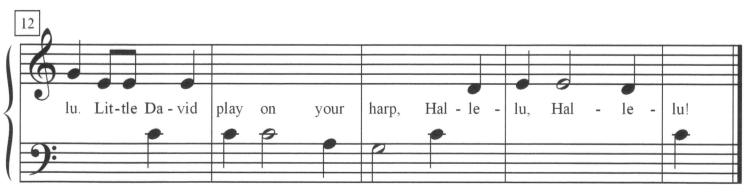

lu. Lit-tle Da - vid play on your harp, Hal - le - lu, Hal - le - lu!

* *Hallelu* is an abbreviation of Hallelujah.

Duet Accompaniment

Clementine

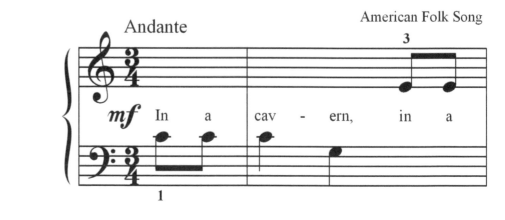

Andante

American Folk Song

mf In a cav - ern, in a

can - yon, Ex - ca - vat - ing for a mine, Dwelt* a

Duet Accompaniment

mf

Teacher's Note: If the pupil is in the early grades in school and has not yet had fractions, do not attempt to explain the dotted quarter-eighth note pattern. The rule to follow is this: *experience should precede explanation.* Teach the rhythm by rote. Delay the explanation until the situation arises at a later time when the student has acquired fraction readiness.

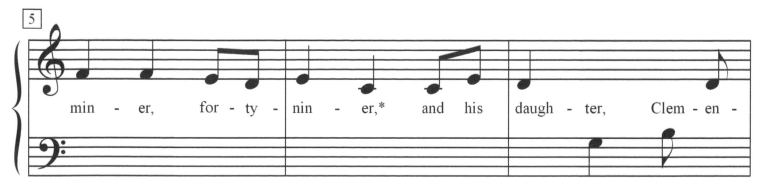

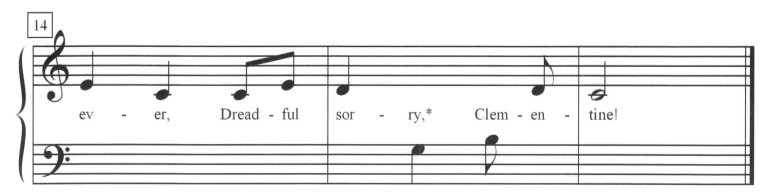

* Dwelt = lived. *Forty-niner* refers to the year 1849, when thousands of men went to California to search for gold.
Dreadful sorry = [I'm] very sorry.

Duet Accompaniment (continued)

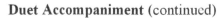

Streets of Laredo

Western Cowboy Song

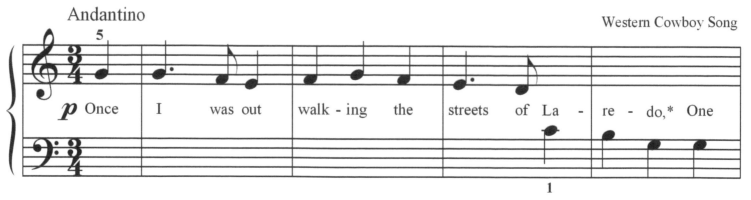

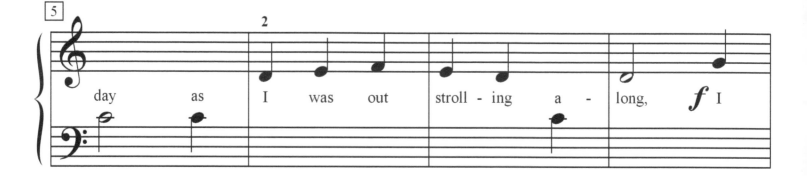

* *Laredo* is a town in southern Texas on the border with Mexico.

Duet Accompaniment

Wait for the Wagon

R. B. Buckley

It's ev - 'ry Sun - day morn-ing, When I am by your side, We'll jump in - to the wag - on and we'll take a mer - ry ride. So wait for the wag - on, Just wait for the wag - on, We'll wait for the wag - on and all take a ride.

Duet Accompaniment

18

This Old Man

Goodbye, Old Paint

Andante

Western Cowboy Song

Good - bye, Old Paint,* I'm a - leav - in' Chey - enne.* Good -

bye, Old Paint, I'm a - leav - in' Chey - enne. I'm

leav - in' Chey - enne. I'm off to Mon - tan - a. Good -

bye, Old Paint, I'm a - leav - in' Chey - enne.

* *Old Paint* is the name of the cowboy's horse. *Cheyenne* is the capital city of Wyoming.

Duet Accompaniment

Had Me a Cat

Allegretto

American Folk Song

Blow the Man Down

* A *chantey* is a song sung by sailors as they work.

Big Rock Candy Mountain

Allegretto

American Folk Song

f On a sum - mer day in the month of May, A___ stur - dy lad came

hik - ing. *p* Down a shad - y lane, through the sug - ar cane, He was

look - ing for his lik - ing. *f* As he roamed a - long he

sang a song of the land of milk and hon - ey. *p* Where a

Duet Accompaniment

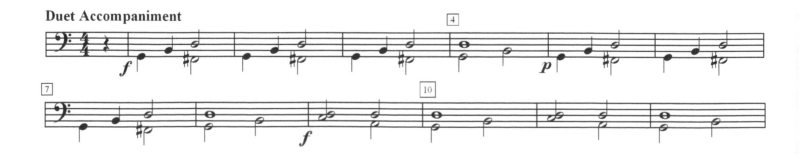

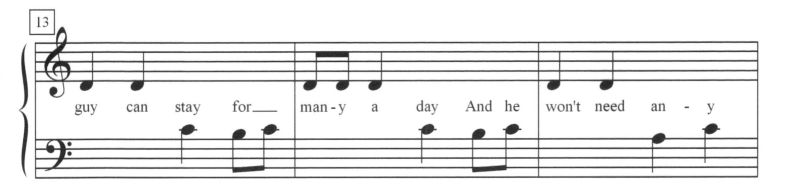

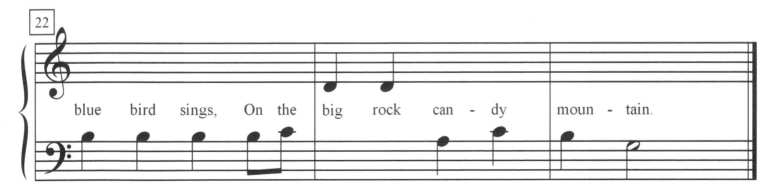

Duet Accompaniment (continued)

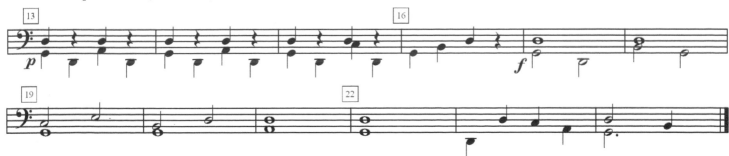